CONTENTS

FORWARD

Why a book about such a thing as frugality? Because the time is right, *right now!*

In the United States of America, collectively we live in an economy of such material prosperity that it's easy to lose the profound impact it has on our lives. The material bounty we have now, have had all our lives and expect to possess in the future is an unprecedented boon in all of human history! Yet, we barely can imagine anything different.

Let's step out of ourselves for a minute. Step into the life experience of most of human kind through out all time. Material living was much more basic than we can imagine. The typical human experience was living hand to the mouth and little else. The concept of having anything to waste, or of saving for a time of retirement was not a part of anyone's life. There were no safety nets. Frugality was not taught, or even spoken of. It just was. It meant survival…or not.

Today, our way of living is a paradox. Our prosperity means we don't have to live frugally. Many of us don't even know the word "frugal" let alone understand the philosophy. But, here is the paradox. The use of a frugal lifestyle is *most powerful when times are good.* Even with the ups and downs of the stock market, right now times are great! Most wealthy people understand this concept very well; that's one reason they're wealthy. **Now is the greatest opportunity to eliminate**

waste and have a real chance to save substantial amounts of money. Frugality is not just about survival anymore. It's the best way to get ahead financially.

So, this book is written to do two things. To affirm and encourage those who already know about frugal living and get "it"; and to influence those who don't know about it and don't get "it." Perhaps those who already know "it" will be reminded of times past when they or their parents or grandparents faced hard times and won, that they will want to break through the wall of materialism that has grown up around their children and grandchildren and use this little book to influence a change. Perhaps....

INTRODUCTION

Without exception, I'm not aware of anyone who does not desire nor would not accept more money than they have now. Actually, most people dream, plan, study, scheme and even gamble with what they have to secure more money. It seems that everyday, a new get rich quick scheme is advertised on late night television, always with the promise of lots of money coming your way, acquired with little or no work so you can live a lavish life style–with money to burn! The truth is, most of us are already "burning" enough money to keep us from our material dreams and goals, and we don't even know it!

Not so long ago, during the 1930's, the entire world population faced an economic crisis that challenged nearly everyone to pinch every penny until it squeaked, just to survive. The Great Depression of the 1930's was anything but great. Devastating poverty shattered the family structure and challenged the human spirit on a scale unequaled in peacetime. To avoid extinction, people honed timeless frugal skills that proved once and for all that a penny saved *is* a penny earned, and since so many were unemployed, that was the only way to earn a penny.

To speak of such recent history today will likely put anyone under 65 years old into a yawning fest, followed by all the jokes about grandpa "remembering when….". However, even though grandpa's stories may be stale, and the old

The Lost Art of Frugality
A Frug's Philosophy

by Solomon Shepherd

THE LOST ART OF FRUGALITY

Published in Austin, Texas, by HCL, Inc.

HCL, Inc.
10 Sunset Trail
Sunset Valley, TX 78745

Unless otherwise noted, scripture quotations are from the *Holy Bible*, New Living Translation, copyright © 1996. Used by permission of Tyndale House Publishers, Inc., Wheaton, Illinois 60189. All rights reserved.

Note: This book is designed as a guide to, and overview of the practices of a frugal lifestyle. It should not be a substitute for sound financial planning advice from a professional. The author has made every effort to provide accurate information and honest opinions. However, there is no guarantee of accuracy or specific result for any individual situation.

ISBN: 0-9718040-2-8

Printed in the United States of America

fashion lifestyle boring in comparison with today's high tech pace, a profound, powerful wisdom is nearly lost to younger generations. That wisdom is the practice of daily frugality. **"Frugal"**—just saying the word sounds strange. What does it mean? What can it do for me?

The dictionary defines *"frugal"* as *"reflecting economy in the expenditure of resources. It suggests a husbanding of resources by living simply and cutting expenses, of habitual savings and avoidance of waste."* What can frugality do for you and me? Accepting frugality as a philosophy and implementing it daily may well be the **most profound decision you make affecting your material life on this earth!** An overstatement you say? Only those who are slaves to waste and want will disagree.

This little book will challenge you to calculate and consider the actual cost of all of your habits of spending and consuming. The key words are "your habits." As most people grow older, they find the habits they chose in their youth either serve them well, or haunt them later in life, begging to be replaced. The joy of choosing to be a "frug" is not to be a greedy skinflint, always looking to cheat others, but discovering the magic of good stewardship coupled with regular saving and compounded interest.

Becoming a true frug puts you in the best of company. Frugs learn how to provide for themselves and so many others. Frugs shun waste while spreading their resources across a broad economy, paying a fair market price. Frugs don't borrow, they lend. They don't take, they give. They are stable, content leaders. They acquire capital, they innovate and they create jobs. They are the most important people in the world. They get along, no matter what.

Does this sound like you? If not, why not? It's easy to do. The first step comes by realizing a basic truth about being human. Your body and mind have a constant battery of urgent appetites that continually call, cry and beg to be fed, always with a promise that if they are ever satisfied they will provide true happiness. The truth is, as you constantly feed these appetites, there is only the temporary halt of the urgent hunger and never sustained satisfaction. Those who seek their happiness by eating, or buying, or driving, or looking good or courting others, or any other attempt at satisfying the flesh, will pay a high price for a continually elusive contentment.

Since the body is always hungry and never satisfied, where *can* you find real contentment? In my opinion, real happiness comes in your spirit - not your body. Spiritual contentment is free. Trying to satisfy the body can be very expensive. But it doesn't have to be. The body's appetite can be fed very economically or astronomically. You decide. When the flesh calls out for pleasure, you can be the slave or the master. (By the way, master is the better choice!)

This little book is easy to use. Read it and along the way, as you start to absorb a frug's philosophy, apply as many money saving tips and eliminate as much wasteful spending as you can. Then periodically, calculate how much savings you have gained by making these changes. Then become a "super frug" by committing the saved money to a powerful investment tool like a Roth IRA that will grow and grow with compounded interest. The numbers will astound you! You'll also have lots of money that used to burn a hole in your pocket....

Let's get started.

Part One:

Thinking about doing the "Frug"

PREPARATION

Things happen for a reason. There's a reason you're holding this little book and reading these words. Clearly this book is not great literature, or a complete "how to" self-help manual. What it is intended to be is an outline of and an advocate for a simple philosophy. A life style opposite of what is popular and prevalent today.

In many ways, this book is iconoclastic to a world that worships at an altar of materialism. It will challenge you to start a positive rebellion against the status quo. In preparation for you to contemplate this way of life, I refer you to a very popular parable from the Bible, not necessarily for religious reasons, but for the power of the illustration Jesus used.

It is a story of a farmer at planting time, scattering seed across his fields. Some seed fell on a footpath, where the birds came and soon ate it up. Other seed fell on shallow, rocky soil that sprouted quickly, but wilted and died quickly as well for lack of nourishment in the shallow soil. Seed also fell among the thorns that choked out the tender shoots that failed to produce a crop. But the farmer had carefully prepared most of the field and as he scattered seed in the fertile soil, the crop that was produced was a hundred times as much as was planted! Jesus ended this word picture saying, "Anyone who is willing to hear should listen and understand."

Jesus was making an appeal for your salvation, but my

appeal for your ears to listen is for the benefit of your life on this earth, facing a fickle material existence.

I contend if you have never contemplated living a frugal life, you have an exciting choice to make. I ask that you redeem the time spent reading this book by preparing your mind to be fertile soil, ready to reap a great return. It will cost you nothing, yet will give you plenty all of your days.

WISDOM

This little book is not a "how to" book. Rather it's a philosophy book. In researching this writing, I gathered lots of books on how to save money, shop better, eat cheap etc. You'll find many of them listed in the resource guide at the end of the book. All these books begin with the same assumption, and that is—*everyone accepts the notion that saving money is good, wise and obviously more desirable than squandering money.* Well I don't believe that philosophy is so obviously instructed or accepted by many people today. It has been replaced by an extreme level of narcissism and materialism resulting in a paradox of workaholics with very high incomes coupled with crippling debt and rampant bankruptcy!

What is missing? I believe its wisdom. Most scholars would agree that King Solomon was the richest man ever in all of history. He owned cities just to keep his horse and chariots. He received more than 25 tons of gold a year. He had so much gold, silver had little value. Yet, at the beginning of his reign as king, it is written that in a dream, God offered Solomon whatever he wanted—a proverbial "one wish" to be granted by God Himself. What did he ask for—long life, money, power, land? No, he asked for *wisdom*. God was so pleased with his response He gave Solomon greater wisdom and understanding than any one has ever had or ever will have. God also promised him riches and honor.

My point is not to bring you to Solomon, but to bring you to seek wisdom. That's a very broad charge, but that's OK. Wisdom is many things, but there are also many things it is not. It is not foolish, weak, false, wasteful, risky, evil, selfish, or arrogant.

When I witness the spending and consumption habits of many people today, I see a high level of foolishness, wastefulness and selfish lies that risk the very ability to survive financially. Perhaps you've been there when a credit card was used in excess with no ability to pay the balance, or a new car was purchased just because the salesman got the monthly payments low, or someone decided they could only wear new designer clothes from the mall or they didn't like to cook so they could only eat in restaurants. Were you there? **These habits of behavior profoundly affect one's entire life.** The great irony is that the person that seeks wisdom in living learns frugality and like Solomon, gains riches and honor as well. Frugal people don't go without. They just learn how to set goals, work hard, be patient, and practice self-control, and in the end, gain true material wealth, not the false "gain" that borrowers pretend to have. Never forget, anything you buy on credit doesn't belong to you. Are you listening? That new car, fancy house, or big TV doesn't belong to you if still owe the bank for it; the bank owns it!

So, I implore you, decide right now, that you will seek to be wise in all you do, especially in regards to spending money. I assure you, you will be happier, more secure and able to help others if you do.

"How can I be wise?" you might ask. There are many

roads to wisdom, but they are all similar. Most wise decisions have been written about proverbially. Learn to recognize the wisdom in the proverbs. For example: rarely is a wise decision made quickly or impulsively or, "Haste makes waste." It's unwise to squander money on things you don't need or, "A penny saved is a penny earned." It is wise to be prepared to work hard for what you have or, "Early to bed, early to rise, makes a man healthy, wealthy and wise"!

Learn to trust the wisdom of the ages. Read a copy of Poor Richard's Almanac and the book of Proverbs in the Bible. Learn to admire successful people and mimic their habits. Learn very early in life that things and people rarely offer lasting happiness by themselves. Personal peace is attained on a spiritual level and happiness with and enjoyment of people and things comes secondarily. Check it out and see if I'm not right.

THE BEST THINGS IN LIFE ARE FREE – CAN YOU BUY THAT?

It used to be easy to get everybody to automatically agree with a few things and "The best things in life are free" was one of them. When you would say that, everyone would think about the splendor of a sunset, or the promise of a new day at dawn, a baby's smile, even the air we breathe and the hope of a long life in good health.

My, how things have changed. For many people caught up in a philosophy of materialism, the best things in life must be *purchased* and be *expensive.* I'm especially troubled by the notion that the best things are always a little more extreme than the last thing that got my attention. From movies, television, advertising, sports, video games, music and even so called "news" coverage, we're becoming more and more numb, so we must be shocked to get our attention and "feel" entertained. We assume the best things in life must be *extreme* and *shocking,* because everything else seems boring.

If you can relate to what I just described, I urge you to step back and examine where this obsession might have its conclusion. I contend that to have the need to be shocked, thrilled, and entertained on an ever extreme level is very expensive, never ending and quite risky.

By the evidence of a created world ablaze in color and clouds at sunset, I know—**"The best things in life are free."**

THE JOY OF CONTENTMENT

Life is full of troubles and problems. Things rarely go as you planned. A man named Murphy discovered a new law. "Murphy's Law" says everything that *can* go wrong will go wrong. Some people have called Murphy an optimist, because it's much worse than that!

The truth is, life is hard, and then you die. So, what's the point of living? Before you start to plan your suicide, let me get to the joy.

We were all created as independent, free agents with a will of our own to decide on our own what our outlook on life is and will be. Once you recognize that fact you begin to know the very real power you possess, all in choosing your attitude about your short life on this earth.

Just where does this power exist? Some would say in your brain, or your "heart" or the alignment of the moon and stars at your birth determined it. I believe the power to be joyful or miserable, happy or sad, at peace or in turmoil, exists in your tongue.

Yes, the power of the tongue is profound. **What we say really matters.** Some of the best descriptions of the power and influence of the tongue were written by the brother of Jesus, recorded in the Book of James in the Bible. He likened the tongue to the rudder on a boat. The small, but guiding influence on a great ship, that could steer to disaster on the rocks or safe harbor in a port. Or the tongue is like a spark that could set a whole forest on fire. We've all witnessed a careless comment or some vicious gossip that tore family apart or ruined a close relationship.

So, you've decided to seek wisdom for it's many blessings, right? What's the wise way to deal with this powerful "rudder" of your life or flame that can consume you or serve you well? The first thing to learn is *self-control*. Self-control—such a wonderful concept, yet quite difficult to accomplish. Self-control is valuable in all aspects of living with our voracious appetites, but it's absolutely vital in how we speak. The key to gaining self-control is learning the truth about it and that truth is- self-control is accomplished on a spiritual level, or as the Bible calls it, one of the "fruits of the Spirit." These "fruits" given to us in spirit are "love, joy, peace, patience, kindness, goodness, faithfulness, gentleness, and *self-control!*" NLT It's very difficult to possess these attributes in our character without growing spiritually. But the beauty is, once you've realized the spirit in you and have decided to accept the mysterious, yet profound truth to be found, the benefits are unlimited.

The "contentment" part of this truth I'm sharing with you is about two steps beyond mere self-control of the tongue. It's about truly being content in all circumstances and situations, choosing words and a speaking style that exemplifies the joy of just being alive. To be able to bring a calming peace to the inevitable and inherent problems of daily living is more valuable than a paycheck, as rare a diamond, and far more attractive than any super model. It can make you the most powerful person in the room.

So let's work on your own recipe for contentment in your life. Start by making peace with your parents, no matter how you were raised. That one thing alone will put you well on the road to peaceful living. If you forgive them for any mistakes they might have made raising you, you will be the one that receives the greater blessing.

Next, test the power. In your next crisis, keep your head, think about and speak of joy and gratitude for your life instead of grumbling or cowering in fear. Be ready for the troubles because you know they're coming. Look at every trial and tribulation as an opportunity to grow in spirit, knowing that it is only on a spiritual level that true happiness can be found.

Learn to not worry. Being concerned, being cautious and problem solving are not the same as worrying. Worry is a worthless, destructive emotion that can change nothing and can only destroy your peace and joy. Resolve to recognize worry early and get rid of it quickly. The apostle Paul wrote this in Philippians 4:6-7 "Don't worry about anything; instead pray about everything. Tell God what you need and thank Him for all He has done. If you do this, you will experience God's peace, which is far more wonderful than the human mind can understand." NLT

As you start to grow in the spiritual part of you, it is then you will find the tree of life that is loaded with the wonderful ripe fruit ready to be picked and eaten—the spiritual fruit that will allow you to be content with your life *no matter what!*

CHOOSING A FRUGAL ATTITUDE

As defined before, basic frugality is the elimination of waste in spending followed by careful economy of all spending.

In theory, the beneficial results are profound. But as usual, the devil is in the details. Often, people think they are frugal, and in much of their behavior, they are. However, it's easy to hold on to one or more "non" frug habits that are like the proverbial "hole in the dyke" that can easily create financial headaches. It's important to always be on the lookout for such leaks.

The truth is, there is no one-way of "being" a frug, but many. Also, frugality is the greatest blessing when it is set as a goal and sought after with your free will. Don't be deceived – tough financial times often are right around the corner and can drag the unsuspecting and unprepared kicking and screaming into forced frugality.

When forced into frugality, people feel victimized and deprived of the perceived comfort their wasteful lifestyle required. The only light of day they hope for is a recovery from whatever caused the loss of income, so they can to return to old ways of waste and excess.

The frug's attitude I'm encouraging you to seek is one that you choose strictly on it's merits and because it benefits you personally. Yes, I want you to decide to be *very selfish* about your money. Not greedy or idolatrous, but very guarded and yes, selfish. Start to realize that the money you acquire in your life is a wonderful blessing, but its source is at best, fickle and very possibly temporary. It is folly to believe otherwise. It is a lesson of life in the material world that you can learn the hard way, or be prepared for in anticipation, which by the way is a great way to be wise (remember wisdom?).

During the Great Depression followed by World War II, frugal living was an absolute necessity for most people. The depression brought unemployment rates of 20%-30%, at a time when public assistance and unemployment insurance were non-existent. Soup kitchens were the last band-aid to avoid starvation for thousands. Many husbands and fathers abandoned their families and set out on foot or rode the rails in search of any work, anywhere to send home to their weary, starving wives and children.

World War II brought relief from unemployment as the armed forces enlisted and drafted everyone fit for battle and the U.S. geared up to feed and supply much of the world with every kind of weapon and fuel. The paradox was, people had money, but material goods were in short supply, so tight rationing became the reality for everything from meat and sugar, to gasoline and tires. These were very tough times! Nearly every one alive then had to learn some basic lesson about frugal living, just to survive.

But they did much more than survive. The collective

spirit of that generation thrived in extreme adversity and deprivation. They met and beat the enemy of poverty. Then they dusted themselves off and whipped Hitler and the worst axis of evil the devil had ever devised on this earth. It wasn't easy. But that spirit of victory carried the U.S. and much of the war weary world to the greatest prosperity and technological advancements in all of human history! We're still riding "America's Greatest Generation" wave of courage of today!

This little history lesson is included for two specific purposes. First, the frugality forced upon that generation *proved* the power of a frugal philosophy and lifestyle. Without out a doubt, when you have not, you make do. Second, I contend that living the frugal lifestyle has nearly unlimited potential for material benefit when *voluntarily chosen and completely embraced during a time of prosperity* as opposed to forced frugality during poverty. That's what lifted our economy so quickly after WW II. My grandparents never abandoned frugality just because the hard times were over. They saved and built and continued to work hard. They built the foundation of today's prosperity by their lifetime commitment to frugal behavior.

It's time for a new generation to learn the truth. It's time to be selfish for the right reasons. It's time to know the world is full of opportunities but also of snares that are ready to eat up all of your money. It's time for you to decide on an attitude that will serve you well. This decision will impact you, and as in the case of America's Greatest Generation, many generations to come—your children and grandchildren!

Choose wisely.

WHAT YOU DO MATTERS A LOT!

"If there's a fork in the road, take it," said Yogi Berra, one of the great philosophers of our age. I'm not quite sure I know exactly what he meant, however, I do know that there are many forks in the road and you can't follow every path to it's conclusion. There are many opportunities and decisions we all face everyday and each decision we make has a profound impact on the outcome of our lives. Don't be fooled by some catchy phrase like "It's all good!" to brush aside the importance of day-to-day decisions. What you decide to do every day matters a lot.

It really matters if you smoke, or lie, or pray, or drive fast, or overeat, and *especially if you start saving money for retirement **at an early age!***

Most of us follow basic human behavior patterns. If you're under 25 you are possibly in an "invincible/immortal" stage, characterized by an attitude that you will be forever young, your life will never change and you will never die. Now when we really stop and think about it, we all know none of those ideas are true. But there is a seduction of youth that lulls us to behave as though they were true for varying periods of our life.

Since you're reading this now, and I have your

attention, I want you to be sure and get this—**you will get old, your life will change many times and in every way and you will likely live a long time as an old person and then die.**

So, with that understood, in your mind project yourself forward in your life to a nice age for slowing down your work and doing all the things you want to do when you have the time —it's called being "retired." Years ago, the U.S. Government set up Social Security to keep old folks from being dirt poor when they retired. Some employers did the same with worker's pensions. The trouble is those plans don't provide much income and they are vulnerable to financial changes in the economy that make the poor old folks get poorer by no fault of their own resulting in the dreaded label of "living on a fixed income". There's also a strong likelihood that today's workers in their 20's and 30's may never receive full benefits from Social Security because the system will be bankrupt or severely changed in a few more years.

I say forget about all that. Don't expect the bureaucrats to be wise enough to give you security in your old age. Take the fork in the road that's staring you in the face right now. Make the decision that matters a lot, and decide to provide for yourself in your last years. Decide right now to open a Roth IRA with the help of a competent financial advisor, and make regular contributions to it the rest of your working life. If you're frugal in your spending and eliminate your wasteful spending, you'll have plenty of surplus to set aside.

Then watch the magic. The power and beauty of the Roth IRA is that you will be investing money now that has been income taxed when you earn it, *but all the interest it earns over* *the years comes to you completely <u>untaxed</u>* when you spend it in retirement. It's called the "magic of Compound Interest." That means that all the interest earned today is added to your savings contributions and then the interest starts earning interest as well. This way of savings is a lot like making a little snowball and then slowly pushing it downhill. It starts out very small and insignificant, but eventually will grow larger then proportionally larger and larger until you can't stop it and it ends up as an avalanche. Look at the calculation table in the reference section to see just how big your snowball will get over the years with faithful contributions and compound interest.

Just a word about my using "a millionaire retirement" as a goal throughout this book; it is used mostly to get your attention. It's an attractive goal, but not necessarily desirable or attainable. It doesn't matter. You don't need $1 million to retire well. It's not that you get rich, but that you learn to pay yourself while you're working and not spend all your money. I propose you try to save 5% to 10% of all your income for retirement. If it's $2000 a year, fine; if it's $5000 a year that's even better. The beauty is, if you start this habit early in your life and never stop, when you retire you'll rest easier! Get good financial advice on where to put your Roth IRA money and start smiling. You are one of the smartest people in the world. If you save $500,000 to $1 million over the next 30 to 40 years, think how much fun it will be to spend and give away that same amount the last 30 years of your life!

That's how this little book can have such a profound impact on the quality of your life, today and many years from now. This millionaire retirement will be financed by money you have right now; the money that's slipping through your fingers and into a fire. That's why living as a frug is for everyone—not just people forced to be frugal out of necessity, but for you, right now!

Part Two:

Actually doing the "Frug"

FIRST THINGS FIRST – STOP THE WASTE!

This exercise is vital for an honest evaluation of your regular spending behavior (habits). What you'll need is a small pocket note pad, a pen and 30 days of regular, normal day-to-day living - not a vacation or during the Christmas holidays etc.

Carry the note pad with you at all times. Use the pen to record every penny you spend. Don't cheat to make it look good. If you buy a $4.50 Latte Grande at Starbucks every day, continue to do so but write it down. Buy a pack of gum? Write it down. Gamble on 5 Lotto tickets for the big $20 million drawing? Write it down. Pay a credit card late fee? Write it down. **Do not change your regular behavior.** This only works if you include all the money you spend, whether paying a bill or discretionary spending.

At the end of 30 days, do some calculating by category such as transportation, meals at home, meals eaten out, snacks, entertainment, etc. Then multiply those categories of monthly expenses by 12 for a year total. Now subtract your current age from 65. Then multiply that number by the yearly expense total. That will give you the total amount you're likely to spend on each category in your working life if you continue in your present spending habits. Pay special attention to the "invisible spending" (the money that goes for the little things you buy without even thinking). That's money wasted—*money that could be working hard for you everyday.*

Let's pretend in one month, I buy 2 magazines @ $5.00 each, 40 cokes (2/day at work) @ .85 each, 8 lotto tickets $1 each, 10 bags of potato chips and 5 packs of beef jerky @ .79 each, a daily paper @ .75 each and a Mocha Latte Grande at Starbucks every Saturday and Sunday morning @ 3.25 each. By my calculation, that's $107.60 a typical month. So, the total for all this stuff a year is…$1291.20. During an adult lifetime, it's **$51,648 tossed into a fire!** Try saving $107 each month from the age of 20 and compound the interest @ 10% in a Roth IRA and you'll have **$680,470 by age 65!** If you continue to earn 10% per year after age 65, you will have $68,000 tax free for the rest of your life - without ever touching the $680,470.00 principle. These numbers should shock you. These numbers should excite you as well! You can accomplish this same degree of turn around in your finances just by stopping the little wasteful spending you do everyday and put that money in a place that works *for* you.

Don't kid yourself. *How you behave with your spending and savings right now will affect your life profoundly.* Cutting out waste is a no-brainer. It's not about deprivation. None of the items on my list of examples are necessities, and most can be replaced with economical substitutes. I make a tasty cappuccino in my own machine for pennies a cup. The same with beef jerky and snacks. It's easy to replace cokes bought from the machine at work with store brands of soda purchased in 3 liter bottles at the grocery. Buying lottery tickets is a self-imposed tax on losers. Magazines and newspapers can be shared or read at the library.

My point is you need to take time to calculate the real, lifetime cost of what you waste, then cut it out and turn it around. A big fat IRA approaching a million dollars by age 65 sounds better all the time. Now get your pen and pad ready and take action.

EVERYTHING COSTS MORE THAN YOU THINK (OR, YOU PAID HOW MUCH?)

When you're shopping, every price tag you see is a lie. The lie is not that you must pay more than the amount on the tag, but that you had to earn 30-50% more than the price just to pay taxes!

The IRS and just about every other tax collector sure got slick when they figured out how to hide their money grab in things like payroll deductions, escrow payments and merchant collected sales tax. Most of us have forgotten that each dollar we earn is skimmed an average of 50% + for all federal, state and local tax obligations! Some tax rebels have calculated that we don't start working for ourselves in a given year until June with every entire paycheck you earn in January through May going to pay for every form of government taxation.

Now I'm not against paying taxes; but it's a fool who forgets how much he pays the taxman!

With this vital piece of information in mind, that makes every $1 bill that actually gets to your wallet worth $2. That means a penny saved is not just a penny earned, but 2 pennies earned. Most people think the way to get more money is to work more to earn more. The best way to get more is to *spend less* every chance you get. So when you eat steak at home for $10 instead of for $40 at the restaurant, you actually saved $60 –$30 in cash and $30 from the taxes you didn't have to pay!

When you keep this important fact in mind when shopping, it really pays to stock up when the price is right. It's a great idea to buy 24 rolls of toilet paper when there's a 2 for 1 special, because there's always a need. When you shop smart and pay a low price for items you really need like food, soap, clothes, cars, insurance, telephone service, gifts and literally everything else you've decided you "need", you can know that the savings you realized is actually doubled.

Here are some pointers on how to shop smart:

1. **Food**—when something is priced at a deep down discount and you'll eat it in the next 6 months (non-perishables or frozen items only), buy as much as you can. When canned goods are on sale in the fall for ½ the price or less, I buy several cases. When a new store has a grand opening and lots of things are priced at their lowest price ever, I buy a lot. In the morning, when most grocery store meat departments have items that need to be sold that day (so the price is reduced for quick sale), I buy steaks at hamburger prices and freeze them. Turkeys at Thanksgiving are virtually given away. I get several so I can serve one at Thanksgiving and Christmas and still have 2 or 3 left for the New Year. I serve lots of eggs at Easter time, when they're really cheap.

2. **Clothes**—I only shop at high quality thrift or second hand-stores or deep discount department stores like Ross or

T.J. Maxx, but only on their clearance racks. I wear some of the finest brand names made in the best fabrics like silk, linen, cotton and corduroy and I never, and I mean *never*, pay more than $10 for any item, and usually $5 or less. Garage sales also offer some great buys. The way it works is, I shop often, but buy only when the item is right for me in size and fashion and the price is low. Then I buy as much as is available. I recently found twelve items at one Ross store in Houston and paid a total of $79, the most I've spent on clothes at one time in years. The retail value was somewhere around $350, or a savings of $271 cash or $542 earned! You can (and should) do it too.

3. **Insurance**—the key is to shop, shop, and shop some more. For life insurance, only buy term life insurance, where you get exactly what you pay for. Whole life insurance is the worst way to try and "save" money. Agents love whole life policies because they make big bucks in commissions. Shop for term life and press the agent for 20 to 30 year level premiums. When you're old, and the premiums skyrocket, cancel the policy and congratulate yourself for not collecting the benefits! Car insurance is a shopping game as well. The best way to save is be a good driver. Speeding tickets really cost a lot in increased insurance premiums. Health insurance can really be expensive if you're buying it for yourself if its not available through your employer. Consider a major medical policy with high deductibles and work hard to stay healthy and accident free. Save the difference on the low premium in a rainy day medical fund that goes to your retirement if you don't use it for medical expenses. Or if you are a Christian, join one of the bill sharing plans listed in the reference section.

The cost can be ½ the cost of insurance and a wonderful way of sharing the burdens with others, while eliminating corporate profits, commissions and waste.

4. **Other Savings**—check out other chapter for savings on car buying, gifts, telephone service etc. The thing you must think of whenever considering buying anything, from a pack of gum to a house, is, "do I really need it and am I willing to *earn* double the price to pay for it?" If you answer "yes," only buy it if you're getting a great price.

BUY THE AMERICAN DREAM AND SAVE A TON OF MONEY

The frugal way to buy almost anything is with cash, with one exception – buying a house. Home ownership is the American dream for several good reasons; the Federal Government allows the interest paid to be tax deductible (which is a form of subsidy), most real estate will appreciate over time, while at the same time provide comfortable, safe shelter for you and your family. Some of the negative aspects of home ownership are; the cost of property taxes and insurance are substantial and inflate your monthly mortgage payment significantly, maintenance and repairs are impossible to avoid and can be expensive. However, overall home ownership is a dream come true for most buyers and a frugal approach can make it all the sweeter.

I'll assume you already have applied the standard frugal shopping behavior and picked out a suitable house for a great affordable price. The decisions you make about your mortgage are where you can literally save a ton of money over the life of your loan. There are two ways to really save. First, if possible, negotiate a 15-year mortgage. This by far, is the fastest way to real home ownership (as opposed to the bank owning your home) and the easiest way to save that ton of money (o.k. the money saved must be in coins to weigh a ton!). You will be amazed at the reduced total pay back of your loan when comparing 15-year to 30-year loans. And, 15-year loans always have a lower interest rate! Check out the calculation tables at the end of the book for some examples of incredible savings when you decide to pay a little more each month for a shorter term on your mortgage.

The other way to save a ton of interest is to put extra money toward the principle each month, thus reducing the length of the loan. This approach works best when done habitually from the beginning of the loan, because during the first half of your loan nearly all of your payment goes to interest while the principle is reduced slowly. The best approach is to make one extra mortgage payment a year, applied directly to the principle. Simply divide your mortgage payment (less escrow amounts) by 12 and add that to your monthly payment, noting that it is to be applied to the principle amount of the loan. This can reduce the pay off of a 30-year note by several years, but really pays off when applied to a 15-year note. You could own your own house in 13 years or less! Then your whole mortgage payment is yours to keep and save.

Check out the calculation tables for the facts and don't miss the chance to really save a ton of cash!

BUYING A CAR

Americans have a love affair with their cars. Cars are truly the symbolic and literal emblems of independence. We like to go where we want, when we want and we like to go in style. In the 1950's and 60's the car makers in Detroit discovered our desire for style in our wheels so they made sure a completely new style of car came out every 3 or 4 years. This was called "planned obsolescence." They sold us lots of new cars this way. But the engines and transmissions in these cars were simple and they didn't run well after 100,000 miles.

Today, cars are much more reliable and complicated but cost as much as most houses did in the 1960's. They are complex, computer controlled and will last 20 years or more and run 200,000 to 300,000 miles if well maintained. Many of today's cars don't even need a tune-up before 100,000 miles!

I've mentioned all this to make the point that used cars are a great value and if you want to be frugal, they're the only way to get a really good deal on a set of wheels.

As a general rule, it's foolish and wasteful to borrow money to buy anything that depreciates in value. Nothing loses value faster than a new car being driven off the dealer's lot for the first time. Before the ink dries on the sales contract, a new car is worth 30% less than you just paid for it! If you don't believe me, try and sell a new/used car for the same price you just paid. People will think you're doing bad comedy and laugh in your face. I've smelled some expensive fragrances at the perfume counter in department stores **but the most expensive smell in the world is the smell of a new car!**

My advice is to always and I mean *always* buy a used car, pay cash and buy from individuals selling their own car. The used market is loaded with great cars that are two to six years old, have between 25,000 and 100,000 miles on them yet will cost only you 20% to 50% of the price of new. I drive one of the most beautiful cars ever made, a Mazda 929. I bought it 5 years old, with 72,000 miles on it and paid $6,500. When it was new in 1994, the car cost nearly $30,000! I only paid 22% of the new price. During the three years I've owned this car I've spent less than $2000 in repairs and maintenance, have driven it 32,000 miles and expect to keep it another 5 to 7 years. There are many similar examples of wonderful cars at low prices. The thing you must do is not settle for anything less than a great deal on a great car. When you go shopping, if you're carrying a big stack of cash in $100 bills to buy a car from an individual, you can really impress a seller to accept your offer. Nobody likes to see a cash deal walk out the door.

So, what do you do if you only have $1,000 to buy a car? I say, buy a $1,000 car and be settled with it for now. Do not jeopardize your ability to save money and never, ever, borrow money to buy a car.

Driving a car that's paid for has lots of other savings opportunities too; insurance is less when you don't have to have all the coverage the bank requires, repairs are affordable because you aren't making hundreds of dollars in car payments, but depositing hundreds of dollars into your rainy day savings account and your IRA retirement fund.

Don't miss this opportunity to be frugal, save lots of money and thumb your nose at the style police.

P.S. It's my opinion that to find the best deals on used cars is to shop for Japanese cars (even though many are assembled in the U.S.). Reliability, superior design, engineering and resale value make Toyota, Honda, Mazda, Nissan, Subaru, Lexus, Acura and Infinity some of the finest rides available. Owners of these cars tend to take pride in ownership and baby them, making them even more desirable. However, they tend to be a little pricey in comparison to U.S. cars of the same year and miles. You should be willing to pay a little more for the likelihood that these cars will run 250,000 to 300,000 miles with basic maintenance and still have good resale value for the life of the car. Still, look for a great price and be patient for the right time to buy—then show up with cash in hand to get your great deal.

THE WORST WAY TO BUY A CAR

If you find yourself being seduced into buying a new car, it's probably because of some smooth talking salesman asked you how much you *could* afford and he worked the monthly payment for that new ride down to that amount. It seemed like he lowered the price, but nothing could be further from the truth!

The latest push to sell new cars is to sell or lease them on a "low" monthly payment. **Don't be fooled!** By lowering the monthly payment, they are only increasing the length of the time it will take to actually own the car. For example, the dealer may say the payments for a $20,000 car are only $199 a month for 5 years. That sounds great! You can afford that, right? But (and this is a big but), way down in the small print there's the truth of this "great" deal. After your 5 years of $199 a month payments, or $12,000 later, you still owe $15,000 on the car. And it's due right now! It's called a "balloon" payment. So, what are your choices then – you either pay $15,000 cash to own the car free and clear, refinance the $15,000 balance and continue to pay monthly, (but your payments will be much more than $199, after all, it's a 5 year old car), or give up and give the car back. But wait, you can't just give it back because you owe $15,000 and the car is only worth $9,000, so you must

share that information with her (Never give this information out, whether you have other offers or not), but if she wanted to make an offer, I would certainly entertain it. She looked at the car thoughtfully and then, to my surprise, she blurted out that she would offer $850! I guess she didn't know that obo means offering a lower price than the asking price. She asked if I had an offer that high. I regained my composure, hid my excitement and told her no, that she had the highest bid. And I told her I would be glad to sell her the car at that price. She was so excited. She handed me the cash and we made the deal right then and there. I laughed and laughed all the way to the bank. I thought I would be lucky to get $600 for that car and so I advertised a little higher to give me some room to come down. Lucky for me, I would get more than my asking price on that little rust bucket!

Be careful when selling your car to an individual you don't know. A good rule of thumb is to never take a personal check for payment for your car. They could easily stop payment on the check as soon as they drive away, leaving you with nothing. Or it could be no good at all – a rubber check. Instead, insist on either cash or a cashier's check from the bank. Always give them a copy of a hand written receipt (you keep the original) as proof of what they actually paid. Buying and selling cars can be fun and beneficial to your pocketbook if you do it right.

EATING YOURSELF RICH

Have you ever stopped to count just how many times you eat? At 3 meals a day—that's 3 x 365 or 1095 meals in a year. During an average life span of 75 years, that equals **82,125 meals in a lifetime.** This one necessity of life gives us the greatest opportunity for daily savings or daily waste. We've already seen what impact saving $3000 a year in a Roth IRA can have. Well here's your chance to "find" the money to fuel your retirement account.

I contend that you are spending an average of $1 more than necessary per meal. It's possible your average waste may be much higher. But take this challenge. Find $21 a week in your pursuit to fill the bottomless pit that your stomach is. If you are responsible for feeding a family, your potential is even greater. If your habits can handle such an adjustment and you get that savings into your IRA, you're a long way to saving $3000 a year and a millionaire retirement.

Here are some ideas for eating yourself rich. Whenever you eat in a restaurant, you can easily prepare 4 meals at home of the same quality, for the same price. When you see a price on a menu in a restaurant, you can know that the cost of the food is actually between 20-30% of the menu price. That is across the board. If you eat T-Bone steaks at your favorite restaurant for $30 a meal, you could serve four T-Bone steaks on the grill at home for that same $30. If you eat hot dogs at a gas station for $1.00, you could do the same at home for less than a quarter. If you have the "eating out only" habit, it's a financial curse! If you can break that habit, even in half, your savings potential is huge. What have you got to lose, but a million dollars?

Once you realize that cooking and eating at home is the way to go, it's time to get good at it. Don't be afraid to get some basic cooking skills. Buy an all-purpose cookbook, like The Joy of Cooking. Ask your friends and family who like to cook to teach you. Most good cooks love to talk about their "secrets." Learn to cook meals you especially like, paying special attention to the good flavors that you particularly enjoy. As the French chefs say, "salt and pepper make the difference." For me it's garlic, onion and chili peppers. Once you get started, I'll bet you make it a hobby that will bless you for the rest of your life, as you welcome your family and friends to your table everyday and on holidays.

Now that you're cooking, the Masters Degree of food savings comes by becoming a master shopper. Grocery stores have changed. They're a trap trying to get your money any way they can. They have a science of how to organize aisles, place things on the shelves, and sell conveniences that will quickly wipe out your $21 savings that week if you're not very careful. There are great shopping bargains in every store, but you have to look hard for them and resist all the fluff. It's important to have the store's current advertising flyer when you go in the store. So, get it out of the paper, or pick one up on your way in the door. This will guide you to most of the best buys that week. One shopping habit that will save you the most is to plan meals *after* you buy what's on sale. To go in to buy very specific items for a recipe can be very expensive! For example, T-Bone steaks are normally $6 to $8/lb., but a 4th of July special may drop the price to $2.99/lb. That's the time to buy several packages for the freezer. Then plan your menu. This plan holds throughout the store. Canned goods usually go on sale in the fall. That's the time to stock up. Ice cream is ½ price on occasion. That's the time to get a brain freeze. One store in our neighborhood sells milk once a month at 3 gallons for $5. I buy 3 and freeze 2, which is a big savings! Remember, never go into a grocery store hungry.

The PhD in shopping savings comes by becoming a Doctor of Coupons. The savings potential by using coupons is limited only to the amount of time and organization you're willing and able to give to the effort. The extreme examples you've seen on TV are real. You can get $200 of groceries for $50 or less. I've never gotten deep into collecting and using coupons, but only dabble in them to save $5 to $10 a trip to the store. If you want to learn from the best, check out Ellie Kay's book in the resource guide at the end of this book and give it a shot.

So, when you're ready to make regular $62 a week contributions to your IRA savings plan, and you start to be afraid to commit to your millionaire retirement, fear not. The savings are there to accomplish your goal when you eat yourself rich, rather than eat Ronald McDonald rich.

BUDGETING

Budgeting is a vital tool and important exercise necessary to accomplish living within your means. Without a budget, all your good intentions are likely to fail.

I'm not going to write a complete chapter on budgeting, because I still have a lot to learn in this area.

I am directing you to a free budgeting guide on the Internet and in my opinion the best expert on the subject. The website is www.crown.org and the expert is Larry Berkett. Get your hands on his budget guide and read his books. Follow his advice and you will be blessed.

ADVERTISING – A FORCE TO RECKON WITH

Advertisers are good at what they do - really good. And what do they do? They cast spells, mesmerize, tempt, beg, cajole, entice, seduce, pressure, entertain and promise true happiness. They would be thrilled to turn us, the buying public, into puppets on strings acting just as they wish.

It is imperative that we learn to resist the power of advertising if we are to attain free agent status in the marketplace. To accomplish this, I start by making peace with advertising.

First, I am grateful for advertising. Advertising dollars pay for many things I enjoy, but would never choose to pay for directly. Things like television, magazines, newspapers, sporting events, radio etc. Even with these benefits, it's vital to resist advertisers' incessant cry for attention and response. I have several techniques as you likely do as well. The important thing is to employ as many resistance techniques as is necessary to maintain control.

I avoid commercial messages as much as possible. I press the mute button, channel surf (much to my wife's chagrin), I leave the room, I look away, and I read, write or give up and turn it off completely. If I can't avoid it, I listen intently to every detail of the language used. I decipher and expose the seduction – and then I talk about it, tell my kids, and spread the word about the techniques of persuasion we just witnessed.

I make a pact with myself that I will purposefully and willfully choose NOT to buy an advertised product, just to send my little message. A good example is how I bought sunscreen for a recent trip to the beach. One brand buys a vast advertising campaign of promotion, complete with Olympic swimmers to sell their waterproof sun block. I recently needed a sunscreen, so as I approached the displays at the store, sure enough, there is the biggest, best display for the brand I had seen advertised so heavily. In their display was every kind of sun tanning product you could imagine, at $12 to $15 for little 5 oz. bottles. But way up on a top shelf, where few people's eyes would gaze, were BIG 16 oz. bottles of a variety of sunscreens with the brand name "NO AD" (no advertising). The price was less than $5 for a bottle 3 times bigger than the advertised brand! A great product, at a great price. I'm all greased up with it right now sitting at the beach as I'm writing this.

There are exceptions to every rule and I make it a point to not throw all advertising in the dumpster. The key approach is to be very discerning and cautious. I am informed by and respond to many ads. I just work hard to make sure I'm in control.

P.S. If you have children, it's vital you help them develop resistance skills at an early age. They are being targeted by some of the most powerful images ever, trying to sell them lots of worthless junk that your kids will try and get you to buy for them.

RMC'S – A BIG TRAP

Recurring monthly charges or RMC's are a huge financial trap that's easy to fall in, and very hard to get out of. Some examples of RMC's; cable television, insurance premiums, long distance plans that have a monthly fee on top of per minute charges, Internet service, exercise/health club memberships, subscriptions to Internet sites, magazines, newspapers and newsletters, charity donation agreements, telephone service (cellular or local in house). All of these "plans" sound quite affordable at the beginning, with offers of "only $4.95", or "just pennies a day", as examples. But as these RMC's add up, they very likely end up eating up all your left over cash. Especially the money that could and should be going to the only good RMC—your monthly IRA contribution for your million-dollar retirement!

So, what should you do about such seductions? The first thing you must do is realize that the low, reasonable "price" being offered is a very small part of the actual cost of whatever service or product you're thinking about buying. That $25 health club membership you signed up for so you would get really buff (but quit using six weeks later) is actually costing you $300 a year, or 10% of your millionaire retirement fund. Add to that; $75 a month for cable TV that plays your favorite re-runs every night, $30 for your monthly pledge to public TV, $75 each month for that high speed DSL Internet connection you thought you had to have, and the $25 a month Blockbuster video plan that was going to save you a lot of money. Before you know it, your $300 a month IRA contribution is slipping right through your fingers, and so is your millionaire retirement!

At the risk of sounding old fashion, I am going to make a strong appeal for you to reject what has become a so-called "necessity" in most households and that is cable or satellite TV. Before you freak out and call me crazy, think a minute. How many times have you spent 10 minutes "surfing" cable to find something worth watching and end up falling asleep watching the Crocodile Hunter? How much time do you spend zoned out with the TV on, just to "get your money's worth" out of cable? Do you read books anymore? And what about your kids? How many glazed eyed hours do they spend glued to the idiot box because you buy it and put them in front of it? It could be considered a form of madness and medication wrapped up in one. I say, give it up, especially as it gets more and more expensive especially with additional Pay Per View charges to see something you really want to watch (like Mike Tyson biting someone's ear!). And the fact is, cable becomes a direct pipeline into your house from the sewer of pornography. The decision to dump cable is a slam-dunk, no-brainer for me. Think about it. It will save you many hundreds of dollars a year and set you free from a vast wasteland (and don't forget about freedom for the kids).

Please stop and think long and hard before you sign on the dotted line for anything that is paid for every month forever. Be especially careful if the contract you're about to sign requires you to do direct bank drafts, making the payments seem invisible. Buyer beware! Save that money instead. Buy cable TV when you're old and a millionaire—you'll have the time and money for it then.

GIFT BUYING

It's fun to go shopping for someone else, choosing just the right gift. Gift buying is impossible to avoid. We all have someone we want to give a gift to. So you don't fall into the debt trap when gift buying, here are a few money saving tips:

SHOPPING AHEAD – I look for items on clearance when I shop, looking for neat gifts to set aside for future gift giving. I always need a general gift for a neighbor, a friend's birthday, child's birthday or a small thank-you gift for someone. I keep a bag in my closet with several gifts for any age and occasion. This saves me time and money when a gift-giving occasion arises. I just go to my closet and choose from my own "store"!

I also frequent a favorite bookstore, Half Price Books. They buy used books, videos, CD's, etc from their customers and resell them. They also have brand new items to choose from, for about ½ the price of a typical retail chain bookstore. I've found gently used kids' videos that are known favorites, for as little as .98 each! Kids (or parents) usually don't mind that they are slightly used and I can afford to give 2 or 3 for much less than one brand new one. These nickel and dime savings really add up especially if you have a lot of people to buy gifts for throughout the year.

Tired of paying off Christmas debt far into the summer? This year vow to not charge Christmas. I try to buy Christmas gifts as early as the day after Christmas when the big seasonal sales are on and bargains abound. Stores offer sales with savings up to 75% off of holiday or seasonal items. The list of your gift recipients seldom changes, so the sizes for next year can easily be guessed. At such low prices, there's every reason to get a jump on next year's gift giving. And when I buy a gift for 50-75% off the retail price, I give a gift that is worth about $20 to 25 and only end up spending $5 to $6 for it. Also, look for stores advertising their grand opening or a big clearance sale. Just don't get caught in the trap of buying more, closer to Christmas because you're got such great deals all year long.

Kids toys can also be bought at a used toy store. This is especially beneficial when the children are toddlers and they only play with the toys for a short time. These stores often have large toys like Playskool picnic tables, play scapes, kitchen sets, etc. Then, when your kids have outgrown these, clean them up and resell them back to the store. If your community doesn't have one of these toy consignment stores, think about being a real entrepreneur and starting your own.

A great way to give a lasting memory to any child you love is to buy a book (a frug will get a gently used one) and then tape record yourself reading the book onto a cassette tape. Be sure to ring a bell or chime to indicate when to turn the page. Give the book and tape to your loved one and they will be thrilled to hear your voice while following along in the book as they "read" their favorite story!

Instead of spending lots of money on greeting cards that are quickly read and dismissed, here is a unique way to give your card and gift for a wedding or graduation. I simply keep the announcement (and the inside envelope) that was sent to me. It's an extra bonus if they left the inside envelope unmarked. But if it has your name on it, use white out and address the envelope back to them. It will not have a gummy seal, so use a glue stick to seal it. There is usually a blank page on the inside of the announcement, so this is where I write my appropriate congratulatory comment and then I send their announcement back to them (as my card) with my gift or money. If they sent out all their announcements and forgot to save one as a keepsake, this one will be even more special. Someone did this for my daughter's graduation and we all grinned in surprise to see her announcement sent back to her! Just calculate all the money you will save by not ever buying another graduation or wedding card again.

NOTE: A frug will *always* reuse wrapping paper and bows, even at someone else's party (especially if they're throwing them away!) And don't forget the Sunday funny papers as a fun way to wrap a large gift!

TRAVEL

My favorite coffee table book is an Atlas. Whenever I hear the name of a place, I want to find it on the map and dream of going there. The chance to pick-up and go to a spot on the globe far away from home is a thrill in my heart. It's also a great opportunity to be frugal.

Traveling can be a very vulnerable time for your wallet, especially if you carry credit cards. So, it's most important to approach the planning process as a frug.

One of the best ways to go cheap is to find a great destination close to home. That will save money and time, both precious commodities when on the road.

Two of the biggest money drains while on the road are eating and sleeping, so plan ahead. For eating, the same rules apply when at home—prepare your own food, drink and snacks ahead as much as possible. Decide before you leave, not to buy snacks and drinks at gas stations, when homemade cookies, trail mix, and carrot sticks in a cooler, with juice, soda and water are handier and 10 times cheaper.

When I go to a new place, my favorite thing is to eat at unique local restaurants. To do this frugally, I plan it as a special event. I avoid spending the "food fund" on the same old boring food found on every street corner in the world (Why someone would travel to Japan and eat at McDonald's is beyond me!). When planning my special meal out on the town in a new place, I'll ask locals for suggestions, read local reviews, drive by, and look at menus before I decide where I will spend $20+ on a meal. The rest of the meals will likely be bought at the local grocery, placed between two pieces of bread and eaten just to fill the hole in my stomach. I expect to save $10 to $15 per person per day eating this way. I'll use that savings to do something special, like deep-sea fishing, whitewater rafting, horseback riding or pay for some other one in a life time experience I'll remember forever (I'd never remember a meal at the local Pizza Hut!).

Deciding where to sleep is another chance to break or save your travel budget. It's easy to sleep well in a fancy place with all of the amenities, but it sure will cost you. When making a road trip, some alternatives to a $60 to $100 pit stop with the family are; have a vehicle set-up for sleeping like a van. Have two or three drivers alternate sleeping and drive through the night (saves money *and* time!). Plan to bunk with family or friends who live along your way, network with churches or travel clubs for a place to crash or park for a night. If necessary, stop at a motel, but choose one strictly for price if you're arriving late and leaving early (these are often a few miles off the highway in small towns, run by families). Camping is another great, vast alternative and will be covered later.

Air travel is a favorite time saving way to travel, but the cost of two different tickets on the same flight can vary many hundreds of dollars! Careful comparison-shopping for your tickets is a frugs playground with big money saved as the prize. There are several ways to find a seat on a plane that's 10 times cheaper than the one next to you. The key is to not settle for anything but a bargain, or else you won't fly.

Many people develop close relations with skilled travel agents who will search for you and alert you when a great price is available for your favorite destination. This used to be about the only way to book travel, but the Internet has exploded on the scene. Now each of us has access to incredible airline fares just by searching for them ourselves. You may already know how to do it, because it's no secret, but here's an example of how I've found some awesome deals. The more flexible I am with dates and times to fly, the better the chance at an unbelievable price. I'll start by searching on two Internet sites that will show me a variety of options on flight times and airlines. These are Orbitz.com and Travelocity.com. I put in my preferred dates and see what comes up. That's my starting point. These sites show flight times and it's a real plus if the best price is here. Then I adjust my days of the week to fly to see if the price drops (airlines have no trouble filling planes on Sundays, Mondays and Fridays). Once I've found the magic days on these sites, I take the same search to a site called Hotwire.com and see what their price is. This site is often an unbelievably low fare with the only unknowns being the time of day the flight leaves and the airline I'll be flying. You won't know those details until you actually buy a non-changeable, non-refundable ticket. But being that flexible really pays. Hotwire gives me only one hour to decide to purchase at that price so I hurry up to make my last search. Priceline.com is my last chance to beat the lowest price so far. If I'm ready to say "yes" to buying a ticket, I make an "offer" on Priceline. It's important to remember, if your bid on Priceline is accepted, your credit card is immediately charged, and you own the ticket! So, proceed only when you're sure you want this ticket. The other factor to consider when making your bid is that Priceline will add the taxes to the amount you bid - which can be as much as $50! The fares on Orbitz and Hotwire include taxes and give you an exact price. So to make a bid on Priceline that will actually save you over your best fare, you need to deduct for taxes ($40+ or -), then another 10% to 25%. If Priceline accepts your bid, you know you got a great bargain. If not, they may suggest a higher bid. Before you do that, make sure it's still a bargain after adding taxes and any other fees Priceline won't tell you about until you've bought your ticket (Read the fine print!). My best buys have come from Orbitz and Hotwire, both for airline tickets and hotels rooms. Sometimes the price is so low its unreal, like $170 roundtrip from Texas to Indiana during Christmas week! Have fun shopping but don't settle for anything short of a great bargain, because they're out there.

When dreaming of a vacation a little more exotic than another trip to "Six Flags Over Wherever" or something slower paced than standing in line with a 1,000 other people to see the Grand Canyon, think about crossing the border for your next trip. That would include Canada, but since most Canadians live within 75 miles of the U.S. border, you might think you're still in Michigan or Minnesota, eh? (Sorry youse guys.) I like Mexico! I like to drive past the border towns and the trashy tourist hype to get into real interior Mexico. I speak very little Spanish, but I always try to communicate with my sparse vocabulary and atrocious grammar; somehow between sign language and sheer will to understand each other nearly every Mexican I encounter has a good laugh at my expense and we both learn a lot as we get business done. It helps to have a phrase book and an English/Spanish Dictionary handy as well. It slows down the process (which is a good thing) and helps you both know you're saying "si" to the same thing!

The key to a positive road trip in Mexico is a little confidence and I strongly suggest you buy Mexican car insurance from Sanborn's Mexico Insurance of Bastrop, Texas (512-440-1100). When you do, ask them for a Travel Guide for the best route to your destination. They will send you a travel book written by Mexico Mike. I wouldn't consider driving 10 miles past the border without it. He details every highway, crossroad, bump, and dog in the road, with highlights of each town, festival, hotels, restaurants, RV parks, things to avoid, and all around great advice to head south with confidence and excitement for seeing what's around the next curve. Get your hands on his books and you'll want to get to Mexico too.

Some of my very favorite Mexican trips are: The most spectacular train in the world through the Copper Canyon (5 times bigger than our Grand Canyon!). The train starts in Chihuahua City but be sure and get off at the city of Creel for a stay at Marguarita's hostel. You will then continue to travel to the west coast of Mexico and back and along the way see the deepest canyons, more tunnels and bridges than you can count and just be trilled by the view around every curve. Side trips in the area: Batopilas in the bottom of a canyon (the greatest drive you'll ever make to a most unusual town!). From the end of the railroad on the west coast, catch a ferryboat to La Paz in Baja California for the finest beaches, seafood and deep-sea fishing in the world (all very frugally priced!) A favorite hangout for Americans and Europeans is the little town of San Miguel de Allende. It is the home of several Spanish language schools as well as museums and great shopping. There are many homes where you can rent a room or the whole place quite reasonably. Don't miss the many theatrical and music festivals throughout the year.

Many frugs from the U.S. find Mexico so inviting they stay there a while and really stretch their dollars. It's a great idea, but I encourage you to not be an "ugly" American by always negotiating an extremely low price from people who are already struggling to survive and work very hard for what little they have. As a matter of fact, when I'm in an out of the way, non-tourist area like I've described, (you'll know when you're in such a place because no one speaks English), I often ask the price, "Cuanta cuesta?" and then when they tell me their price I say "no bueno" (or "that's no good"). Then, instead of offering less, I will pay a few pesos more than their asking price. I can usually easily afford it and especially when buying handcrafted goods from the actual producer, I'm truly blessing an industrious worker. Also, when you do this, you'll be very well received as a guest in their community, a blessing for you as well. Try it and see.

The bottom line is; travel is exciting, adventurous, and a little risky but very rewarding. Do it as a frug so you can stay longer, or go more often or just get more travel for your money. The rewards will live a lifetime in your memory and pictures.

CAMPING – THE BEST WAY TO GO ALMOST ANYWHERE

The title of the chapter is my opinion. Many people disagree with that opinion and they know who they are (so you can skip this chapter if you want).

But I believe travel by camping is a blend of many of the best things in life, the greatest being the opportunity for extreme frugality! Other wonderful things about camping include; making lifetime memories (some great, some not so great), getting very close to the very best of God's creation, slowing down enough to forget, for a while, about jobs and deadlines, using basic life skills like cooking outdoors, reading maps, building fires and star gazing. Our seven-day week was designed by the greatest mind in the universe with one day of rest, Sunday, and I say a well-planned camping trip is like the proverbial "month of Sundays."

I'm not going to try and "teach" you how to camp, but encourage you if you're not already convinced, to make your way to take the time and find the places where your spirit can step out of time to be renewed. I've camped with every kind of equipment, from everything carried on my back to 12,000 lbs. of home comforts hauled behind a big truck. It doesn't matter how, it just matters that you do it.

There are things that happen in your thinking when you slow down and sit a spell. I'm sure you've found yourself totally mesmerized by the awesome visuals found while starring for hours into the heart of a campfire, studying the eerie way the glow of coals change constantly as flames lick up and dance on the wind. For me it beats cable TV hands down. All this takes place under a heaven blanketed with evidence of billions of other worlds created in at least as much splendor and grandeur as our own. Look up, look down, look all around you and you're in the middle, almost gone, lost in the knowing there is no need to know more, just be a part of it. Where was I? Oh yeah, sitting by a fire. Isn't it great?

Forgive my drifting off, but it's for that drift, camping is the best way to travel whenever possible. So stock up on all the stuff you'll need at garage sales and hand-me-downs from your parents etc. And be sure and use it. Start dreaming of where you can escape to soon; the nearby great park or to a mountaintop in the next state. The mental therapy is free and so much better than psychotherapy.

P.S. Many retired folk find full-time "camping" in their RV's an exciting, adventurous and yes, frugal lifestyle. The freedom of the open road mixed with traveling with all the comforts of home in today's quality recreational vehicle offer retirement years seeing the sights, visiting family and friends all at a very low cost. Find information about "full-timing" in the reference section at the end of the book.

A TRUE FRUG'S VACATION

I once went on a vacation that was probably my most memorable for many reasons!

I was newly married—had little savings and no credit cards. We decided to take a road trip from Michigan to the east coast and had $300 to do it. We went for 10 days, allotting ourselves $30/day for food, gas and fun. Now, remember, this was before the endless opportunities that can be found on the Internet, and vacationing by car was still the cheapest way to go. Looking back it seems impossible that we could actually accomplish such a trip, but believe it or not, we did!

Before leaving, we packed a box of staples & filled a cooler with meats and frozen items out of our freezer and headed out in our '86 Toyota van. We took out the backseats and fit in an air mattress for sleeping. This way we didn't spend a dime on sleeping accommodations. We were too frugal for that! We took along a road atlas and always found a neat camping place in a state forest to sleep for the night. The next day we'd find a state park to shower in. On the east coast, they didn't charge to go in for the day (it might be different now). If we needed some clean under garments, we'd wash them out there and hang them in the van to dry as we drove.

There were days when we drove a lot, consuming a lot of gas. On these days, we had a plan in place to stay on our budget of $30.00/day. We always found a state park, roadside park or picnic area to fix our evening meal on our camp-stove. We never ate hot dogs and chips at the local gas station, but stayed on our budget by fixing pb& j sandwiches on my lap in the car as we drove. We decided to eat dinner out in restaurants only every 3rd day. So on that 3rd day, we would plan our agenda around the area we were in. We would go sightseeing on our bikes and work up an appetite for the anticipated evening meal.

The most memorable part of our vacation was arriving in a quaint part of the Eastern shore of Maryland. My spouse had been reading a James Michener book about this area and it was a goal to see the places written about in that book. As we entered the town, we saw a row of restaurants on the harbor's edge, all advertising blue crab specials. All you can eat! We drooled all over the dashboard as we gazed at the upcoming restaurants, but were reminded that it was not our night to eat out. So, we proceeded to the park at the end of a peninsula. This was the destination we had from reading the book. It was written about so idyllically that we both couldn't wait to eat our "picnic dinner" out there.

SURPRISE, SURPRISE! The book had been written about a time at least 100 years earlier. This place just could not be the same place so beautifully written about in James Michener's book. This park had grass up to my knees with overflowing garbage cans and broken tables and swings.

We were so disappointed but were so hungry we had no choice but to eat on the wobbly picnic table. The most pathetic part of this scenario was our menu. We were almost out of food so we polished off the last of the hot dogs - a little green around the edges (no kidding). The buns were stale, the chips were soft and the soda was flat. We had to laugh to keep from crying. We both wanted to eat crab so bad, but it wasn't our night! Now some of you might be saying, "Forget the 3rd day eating out rule. If we want it, we'll have it, and worry about how we will eat the rest of the trip later." But remember we did not have the luxury of credit cards then, and we were determined not to run out of money before we got home.

Our resolve to stick to our budget seems rigid nowadays and almost unreal to me now, years later. But a fun cheap vacation without credit cards can be accomplished. It sure was fun to go and be a frug; to avoid temptations to buy souvenirs that you can't afford (and don't need). We took rolls of pictures to capture our trip and did all we wanted to. We walked on the beach, hiked, biked and enjoyed lovely meals out on the town (every 3rd day!!). We look back and laugh at our picnic on the peninsula, knowing most people would have given in to temptation and gone over their budget to charge a fancy blue crab dinner. But it felt good (and still does) to know you made memories you can laugh about years later without going into debt. The best part is returning from vacation knowing this trip won't bite you in the pocketbook when the bills come in the next month.

Now start thinking about your next vacation as a frug.

INTERNET

There's a powerful new tool available to today's frug that Grandpa could never even dreamed of during the Depression and it's the Internet. The mysterious, vast, interconnected multitude of computers, glass fibers, phone lines, businesses, government, universities and individuals presents us all with access to more of everything in all the world. The key word is "everything", so the internet is not unlike all else in the material world—it requires extreme self control or you may get sucked into the biggest cesspool in the world and never return.

So...do be careful and learn how to save lots of money when you buy things like travel, used cars, and just about anything you can imagine is selling cheap on the E-Bay auction!

I'm not going to pretend to be an Internet shopping guru, but it's not hard to get started. I especially love getting really cheap air travel tickets for my wanderlust. I mean really cheap—$164.00 round trip from Texas to a little town in northern Michigan, that's 6 flights, less than $28.00 each. My favorite thing is to get a really cheap ticket, find out the flight is overbooked when you're at the gate, and then get chosen to give up your seat for a later flight. You get a free ticket, hotel and meals to travel in the morning. What a deal!

Anyway, back to the Internet. The key, as always, is: BE

A GOOD SHOPPER. And for things you really need to buy. My son's wife "really" needs a very fancy face cream that sells for $50 at department stores. A search on E-bay led them to the same product for $8.00. THAT'S A GREAT DEAL! It's time to stock up. I booked a suite at a hotel in downtown Dallas two days before traveling and paid $54 for a $129 suite. THAT'S A GREAT DEAL! I paid for the rest of the trip (meals, gas etc.) with the savings.

This is not an Internet instruction book, but an encouragement to use this very powerful shopping weapon for your benefit. I use the Internet for very specific purposes only, to avoid allowing another glowing screen to mesmerize me into oblivion and waste lots of my time.

Be careful, be wise and be frugal especially on the Internet.

TOTALLY AVOIDABLE EXPENSES

This subject is so obvious, it's strange to even have to mention it, but reality screams, "Speak the obvious"!

I heard an unbelievable bit of news on the Clark Howard radio show. He said that Blockbuster Video Rental Company had a very ironic set of figures in it's accounting in a recent year. Their profit for the year was almost equal to the total of late fees they collected from all the millions of people who can't return rented videos within the 5 day rental period! Ponder that for a moment... think of the thousands of stores, millions of customers, tens of millions of rentals of other people's intellectual property, literally a vast corporate enterprise, American economic dream come true and it's all built on profit from late fees. I'm not against profitability but it's almost a crime when it's built exclusively on pure consumer waste.

A frug works hard to eliminate waste and promotion of economical use of resources. It's vital to cut out the waste. Here's a little waste cutting exercise; my top 10 list of TOTALLY AVOIDABLE EXPENSES. Feel free to make your own list.

1. ALL LATE FEES (including library fines)

2. TRAFFIC TICKETS (including parking fines)

3. BOUNCED CHECK FEES

4. CREDIT CARD INTEREST

5. BAIL BONDS

6. ALMOST ALL LAWYER FEES

7. INTEREST ON ANYTHING THAT DEPRECIATES IN VALUE (LIKE CARS!)

8. COLLECT CALLS YOU ACCEPT THAT AREN'T LIFE OR DEATH EMERGENCIES

9. WITHHOLDING TAXES YOU GET BACK ON A TAX RETURN CHECK

10. CABLE TELEVISION

ONCE-A-WEEK COOKING

It's Sunday afternoon and just about the only time in my busy week I can expect to have time to do what I like and relax while doing it.

What I did today is an example of what I really like to do —cooking and saving lots of money and time.

For example, we're having guests for dinner, so I pulled some rib eye steaks out of the freezer. I bought these when they were on sale (reduced for quick sale—look for those stickers). I paid $2.99/lb for steaks that normally cost $6 to $8/lb. The store also had chicken leg quarters for $3.90 for a 10 lb. bag (.39/lb.) I cut the drumsticks from the thighs and froze them separately. The drumsticks are a favorite for the kids (a result of good training since childhood). The chicken thighs are very versatile for many dishes. My favorite is to cut the meat off the bone, season with chili pepper and garlic, sauté with grilled onions and peppers for wonderful fajitas. Then I boil the bones with onions, celery, and carrots for a wonderful soup stock. When cooled, separate any remaining meat from the bones, discard the mushy veggies and use the broth and meat for soup. Add rice, noodles or potatoes and any vegetables you like and you have another wonderful meal!

Today I've fired up my Texas grill/smoker and I'm smoking enough chicken thighs to make 5 or 6 meals I'll serve all week, both for lunches & dinners. They make great chicken salad when boned.

I also bought whole chickens at the grand opening of a new store for .59/lb. I'm putting 2 of them on the grill too. I've cut them in half so I'll have 2 whole breasts fully smoked in the freezer tonight, all ready to thaw out for a quick main course when company drops in.

I save even more money when firing up the grill. I start with just a few charcoal briquettes, and then add wood chunks I've collected (for free) from my neighbor's trees. The aromatic smoke produced fills the backyard and makes meat taste heavenly. My favorite is pecan wood, but I also have a choice of oak, apple or mesquite. Hickory is great, but hard to find where we live. So always, be on the lookout for dead limbs of fruit or nut trees to smoke your meat. The important thing is to make cooking fun. Fix the food you like in a way that saves you time and money. You'll eat better than at most restaurants and save lots of money.

You don't have to cook just chicken to save money either. Last Mother's Day I prepared a feast of steak and crab legs, fresh corn on the cob, sweet potatoes and fresh squeezed lime-aid. Four of us ate like kings for less than $30. At a restaurant, 4 plates of steak and crab with all the trimmings plus tax and tip would have topped $130 in my neighborhood. That's some real money saved.

Start planning how you can spend a little time cooking ahead to save tons of money over the years. You'll probably lose a few pounds too, eating healthier.

DON'T FORGET THE FLOWERS!

While visiting with a group of very sweet, very old ladies, I asked if any of them lived through the Depression. They began to giggle, as they all remembered those formative years. One theme became evident as several of them shared their families' saga of survival in dire poverty—in spite of hardship and deprivation, life was good, full of love, and they didn't think they were poor.

One story was particularly powerful. A quiet, dear, octogenarian started her story by saying no one in her family had a job, and they lived literally without money. She continued without hesitation to tell how rich her life was living with her parents and grandparents, as they worked together growing food and flowers with the emphasis on flowers.

She spoke of how her grandmother, in her 80's, carefully gathered seeds each year to plant the next season. The fruit of their labor was a bounty of fine food to eat fresh and preserve for winter. Then with a sparkle in her eye that might have been a tear, she talked of how her mother would pack baskets from their bounty and deliver them to the families they knew who were *really poor.* And yes, the baskets always had flowers in them too.

Gardening may not excite you in any way, but it cannot

be denied how beneficial a well-tended garden can be, both for your health and your wallet. Today's garden may be a few large pots of tomatoes and peppers on an apartment balcony, or a back yard garden with drip irrigated raised beds.

My favorite gardening experience is spending a little money to "pick my own" at a nearby truck farm. (Have you tasted fresh sweet corn cooked just minutes after picking?) I can invest a few bucks at a local farm, and in an afternoon can fill a freezer with fruit and veggies that taste better and cost less than anything in a store.

My favorite way of preserving many fruits, vegetables and herbs is to dry them in a dehydrator. Dehydrators can be found at garage sales, or in catalogs for usually less than $25.00. You don't need a fancy one, just one with a working fan (you can even use your oven set on the lowest setting). I use dried chopped onions for cooking almost daily so onions are at the top of our list to "dry" in our dehydrator. I also like to dry fresh fruit like bananas, apples, pears, etc. that turns into easy snacks to take on hikes, or pack for lunches. Beef jerky is a coveted treat around our house. I buy rump roast when it's on sale, use lots of seasoning, and make the best beef jerky. I have to ration out everyone's portions so we all get a fair amount and then hide the rest for later!

See how much you can save by buying cheap in season, growing your own in a backyard garden, in pots on the porch, or even an herb garden in a window. Better yet, join a community garden and have fun growing and saving with your neighbors. Fresh food is always the highlight of any menu. And don't forget the flowers!

FIELD AND STREAM

I've lived in communities where there is an annual phenomenon. Schools are nearly empty on a school day, businesses are closed on a weekday and nearly every man, boy (and many women and girls for that matter) are dressed in bright, unusual costumes, running around outside in the cold. No, it's not Halloween. It's opening day of deer hunting season!

Hunting and fishing may not be for everyone, but there's no doubt that this earth's bounty of wild game can fill the freezer with some of the best food ever and as is often the case, if approached frugally, some of the cheapest food too.

If you live in a rural area, you probably know about deer season. Deer are so well adapted to our environment and such prolific breeders, it's an absolute necessity to harvest (or hunt) them to avoid them dying of mass starvation and disease. Also, hunting can be one of the most positive activities to relieve stress, build relationships and create family memories. I have no fonder memory of being with my dad than when we were sitting quietly in a deer blind in an autumn woods, bow and arrow in hand, waiting for deer to come along. And guess what? I got one at age 14! It was a marvelous time.

Hunting and fishing can be the way to a feast when there is no food or money. Most of us have money, but can still hunt and fish very economically and fill the freezer with gourmet delights, for pennies a pound.

P.S. Just a word of caution. Hunting and fishing can be very expensive! If you're looking for a frugal food source, you'll be hunting and fishing near your home without spending a lot of money on expensive gear or out of state licenses. Don't be confused; salmon fishing or moosehunting in Alaska is not frugal.

HELPFUL HOUSEHOLD HINTS

Here is a sample list of the many ways to save some extra money. But this list is small compared to all the lists you will find on the Internet, at your local library and in your local newspaper. A frug is always pays attention to new ideas when they come across his path!

1. Don't throw away those Ziploc bags. Instead, turn them inside out and wash with soap and warm water. Air-dry and reuse! By doing this, I only buy one box of each size of Ziploc bags about once a year. I'm not only saving money, but I'm recycling which is good for the planet too.

2. If you have a problem with flies or ants, give them a good spray with cheap hairspray. They will quickly disappear and it's cheaper and less caustic than pesticides.

3. Your expensive candles will last a lot longer if you place them in the freezer for at least 3 hours prior to burning.

4. Don't throw away those old dusty plastic or silk flowers. To clean them easily, just put them in a paper bag with salt. Shake vigorously and the salt will absorb the dust and dirt and leave your artificial flowers and greenery looking new again!

5. Don't buy expensive room scents that plug into outlets and constantly need to be replaced. Do what frugs do: Spray a

bit of perfume on a frequently used light bulb for a lovely scent that appears when the light is on.

6. Instead of costly drawer sachets to scent your linens and lingerie, just place a scented dryer sheet in your drawers or linen closet for a fresh scent.

7. If you grew up in rural America, you probably remember your mom hanging the laundry out to dry in the summertime. It always smelled so fresh and clean and didn't cost a dime. Granted, it takes a little more time, but clothes usually require less ironing when hung to dry. If you own an electric dryer, I guarantee you will save loads (pardon the pun) on your electric bill! The feel of crisp clean sheets off the line can't be beat. Try it sometime and save some money too.

8. To save your Tupperware from staining with tomato products, just spray it first with a nonstick cooking spray. It works great!

9. Tired of being attacked by mosquitoes and not having any expensive spray to cure the itch? Try applying soap to the bite and you will experience instant relief.

10. To avoid medication for common headaches, just try this trick: cut a lime in half and apply it to your forehead. The throbbing will go away.

11. Household uses for Alka Seltzer:

Drop 2 tablets in your toilet bowl, wait 20 minutes, brush and then flush.

To remove stains from a flower vase, just drop 2 tablets in the vase and soak. This also works well for cleaning a thermos bottle.

To unclog a drain drop 3 tablets down the drain followed

by a cup of white vinegar. Wait a few minutes, and then flush with hot water. This is much cheaper than Drano and works just as good.

12. Are you tired of veggies going bad before you get a chance to use them all? Try wrapping vegetables in aluminum foil and they will keep for weeks.

13. Did you know car window cleaner (the kind you put in your car's windshield washer system) is stronger and much cheaper than the window cleaner you buy in a spray bottle for your home? When your bottle is empty, just refill it from a gallon jug of car window cleaner. It does a super job around the house and costs around a buck for a gallon jug.

14. Don't let bloodstains ruin your good clothes. Instead pour a little Hydrogen Peroxide on a cloth and proceed to wipe off every drop of blood. It works every time!

15. Next time you buy a box of SOS pads, take the time to cut them in half. It's much more economical as most of the time you only need a ½ of a pad anyways and then you can throw it away immediately. No more smelly, rusty SOS pads hanging around your sink anymore. It also helps keep your scissors sharp.

16. If your dear children have decorated your walls with crayon drawings, don't fret or resort to costly, caustic cleaners. Just use a damp rag with baking soda, and the crayon will come out with minimal scrubbing. Let the kids help for a good consequence!

TALK IS CHEAP

The telecommunication industry is highly competitive right now, so it opens doors for savings or squandering money. This little chapter is not a complete guide since the landscape is constantly changing. But you can expect to get more talk for a lot less money if you keep looking.

Here are a few targets to aim for when shopping long distance phone service:

1. A very low per minute cost—less than .05 per minute is not unusual.

2. 6 second incremental billing especially important in the first minute.

3. No monthly service fee. This is vital. Companies love RMC's or recurring monthly charges because they never go away and they inflate whatever great per minute charge you think you're getting. Just refuse any plan that has one, period.

4. Check fine print closely. Look for high in State per minute charges and surcharges. Avoid them.

5. For businesses, incoming toll free calls per minute charges should be as cheap as regular long distance. Just keep shopping until you get a great deal.

6. Some smaller companies offer 10% rebates or donations to a charity or ministry of your choice, which is great, but only if you get a good deal to begin with. Otherwise

make your own contributions separate from your phone bill.

7. I avoid phone companies like AT&T that profit from pornography by operating 900#'s and billing for phone sex lines. All your phones should have a block for theses smutty businesses; just ask your phone company for it.

8. Consider if a cell phone with long distance included could eliminate your need for a home phone.

HOW MUCH IS TOO MUCH?

Most of you reading this book live in the U.S. We have so much more than most other nations. We are blessed with choices. We can choose to work for someone else or ourselves, making a decent living either way. We choose where to live —in the mountains, near the coast or in the Midwest. We have many choices that matter a lot, like whether to attend church or not and which one, who to vote for, which school is best for our kids etc. And daily we face almost meaningless choices in our day-to-day living, and that's the point of this chapter.

As we are bombarded by ads, signs and commercials, we have even more choices. Should we give in to the sale signs at the mall, calling us to "save 50-75 % off selected merchandise", or resist the urge to go in and buy yet another swimsuit, dress or sweater that we don't really need? I know young women who've confessed to own 3 closets full of clothes, many with the tags still on them, as evidence of their frivolous spending.

How much is too much? Is it really necessary to own 8 or 10 or even 12 bathing suits (even if you do live near the beach?)? (That goes for sweater mongers in the north too!). It's more frugal (and yes, wiser) to own just 2 or 3 (preferably bought on sale) and wear them out before buying new ones. I know clothes hoarders, shoes hoarders and hoarders of cd's, videos or books. How much is too much? I think it's too much when you have to rent a storage space to keep all of your excess that won't fit in your garage, attic or basement. I remember George Carlin doing a bit in his comedy routine about Americans needing to get bigger houses to store all their "stuff." Don't get rid of anything; just keep getting a bigger house! It's sad but true.

Whether you collect thimbles, or guns, or posters or Ty Beanie Babies, my question to you is: Why and how much is too much? When are you satisfied? Will you ever be? And when you die, think of the lucky relative who will be left figuring out what to do with your vast collection of "stuff."

Think instead of living frugally or lean. There is an article written by a nun who worked side by side with Mother Theresa in Calcutta, India. These dear saints lived the simplest of lives, in poverty, often in the same conditions as those they were helping. This nun wrote that she owned 7 dresses, all identical in color and design. It was the same with their headdresses and undergarments. Imagine 7 outfits all the same – one for each day of the week. She remarked how easy it made her life. No choices or worries abut what outfit to wear that day. (Now I know she didn't need to impress anyone or need heavier clothing for changes in climate, but bear with me on this thought). Imagine freeing your mind of all the clutter that we, (who have lots, thus have lots of choices), get bogged down with. I guess the parochial schools were on to something when they adopted the idea of dress codes. It's freeing not to have the worry about what to wear everyday to school and eliminates fighting among the "haves" and "have-nots." I've often thought of that nun's article and have even tried to pare my wardrobe because of it. It seems foolish to put away my winter clothes when spring arrives and with them all of the sweaters, turtlenecks etc that I didn't wear all winter. But we are a nation of hoarders. So I pretend I'll wear it next year–(for sure)–and save it because I like it, or paid a lot for it and feel guilty for not liking it so much after I bought it. Then next season I put away my summer clothes and on it goes.

Sometime soon in <u>my</u> life I will have one closet full of summer and winter clothes. A few dressy items, a few casual items, and some bum around stuff. Maybe even one day I will own 7 identical outfits and quit worrying about all this "stuff" that really isn't so important in the big scheme of things.

HAVING A BABY

Having a baby is one of the most awesome and terrifying experiences to face a family. There are not enough classes or videos to prepare you for this life-changing event. It can also often be a huge financial burden on a family-but it doesn't have to be. Car seats, playpens, cribs, highchairs are all necessities, not to mention the bottles, clothes, diapers, toys and blankets that babies must have to be content! But don't despair, if this is your first encounter into the world of baby making, these ideas will help you save lots and hopefully inspire you to come up with more on your own.

All of the above mentioned items could be purchased at baby consignment stores. These stores take in like new baby furniture and clothes and resell them for much less than new. If you like to shop at thrift stores or peruse garage sales, you will find almost everything you need to outfit your baby. Garage sale listings in your local newspaper will even highlight their baby items, as these folks know they are coveted items that will draw a crowd to their sale. All of these items will be cheaper at a garage sale or thrift store than the consignment store, but they might not be in as good of shape and may require minor repair and a good cleaning.

A young mother in our church organized a baby item swap day. She advertised to mothers of babies and toddlers, asking them to bring in like new furniture, clothes, toys etc.

that they no longer used. On a Saturday morning expectant or new moms came in and "shopped" for what they needed for their baby. It was free and a great way to recycle all the stuff that's accumulated when starting a family. Then when you're done with all this "stuff," turn around and donate it at the next swap day or give it to an expectant neighbor or friend. This is a frugal way to outfit and entertain your baby.

Cloth diapers are much cheaper than disposable, even with a diaper service to clean them for you. Each area of the country varies in price for this service, so check out your area for the best deal for this cleaning service. Cloth diapers are more hassle, but after your child is potty trained, they turn into the most coveted cleaning and polishing cloths in your home. They are excellent for washing windows and drying your car. They are the only baby item I would not get rid of as my child grew up.

Breastfeeding is arguably the best way to feed your infant. Besides being free, breast milk provides your child with natural antibodies from the mother that protects the baby from diseases and infections that formula doesn't provide. Breast milk reduces ear infections and diarrhea, reduces the chances for Meningitis and childhood Leukemia and lowers the risk of SIDS. Breastfed babies are sick less and go to the doctor 5 times less than formula fed. The colostrums (or first milk produced after birth) are the absolute best for your baby in their first days of life. It's high in infection fighting protein at the time your baby needs it most. It's like your babies first immunization.

The benefits for mom are:

Helps mom return to her pre-pregnancy state (or wt.) faster.

Less pre-menopausal breast cancer

Less likely to develop osteoporosis

Early breastfeeding causes the uterus to return to normal size quicker and minimizes blood loss.

With breastfeeding, there are no bottles to prepare, no mess or expense. Breastfeeding promotes the most special bond between mother and baby. And breastfeeding makes a mother more in tune to her babies needs. There's no better or more frugal way to welcome your new baby into your life and the world.

All in all, having a baby doesn't have to "break the bank" within your family. Just break out of the mold and modern day traditions that say your baby must have all "new" stuff; toys, clothes, furniture. You're not going to impress your baby, so who are you trying to impress? Be a frug instead. Your baby will never know it and will likely grow up loving you more because you'll have more money when they really need it, like for college or their first home.

MAKE THE CREDIT CARDS PAY YOU

If someone is in bankruptcy, credit card misuse is likely in the middle of the problem. Our banks are addicted to the astronomical profits being generated on credit card use, so they are very aggressive with their promotions. Banks are targeting kids right out of high school with the goal of getting college students hooked on using credit cards for as many purchases as possible, from tuition and textbooks to pizza and beer. The seduction of easy credit, together with extremely low minimum payments is hard to resist.

But hear me now—**resist you must!** For the person with no self-control and a fist full of plastic, credit cards are the heroin of the money world. But the "high" delivered at the cash register soon comes crashing down into a pit of despair as desperation sets in; one card is used to pay another as the balances due only grow higher and higher as the interest mounts up. **If this is you, something must be done immediately.** Check out the resources at the end of this book and do something about it, right now!

If you're not addicted to abusing credit cards, I've got good news. There are ways they can be handy tools and pay you to use them as well. But a warning, *do not try this if you are weak in this area.* Just skip this chapter.

There is a game credit card companies play with people they consider their best potential customers - people who make good money and have an excellent credit history. They offer these people lucrative incentives to open an account. The incentives include frequent flyer airline miles, discounts toward car purchases, free long distance phone cards and cash refunds. There is only one way the use of these cards and incentives should be attempted, or else it's not a great deal. As with all credit cards, these carry a grace period to pay off all charges and owe no interest. If you are disciplined enough to pay off, without fail, the full balance every month, then the more you use the card, the more you'll benefit from the incentive. The credit card company literally pays you to use their card. Some people will use these cards to pay nearly all their bills and make purchases like gas, groceries etc and before you know it, they've got free tickets to Hawaii! Just remember, this type of credit card use is only for the most disciplined frugs because the seduction is always there to use them for things you can't afford.

GIVING

Being frugal is all about getting more money and keeping it all for yourself, right? A greedy frug would say so, but I think that's dead wrong.

True frugality is about good stewardship and eliminating waste. This great earth is a cornucopia of resources; a horn of plenty, sufficient for all. The greatest enemy of life-giving resources is both greed and waste. They represent a black hole that gobbles up the stuff of life and sends it to another world, inaccessible to people who need it most!

Remember the family earlier in the book that had no work or money during the Great Depression, yet they grew food and flowers in their garden. They managed and tended the good earth for the benefit of their family and then carried their surplus to those in greater need than themselves. I believe they never thought of themselves as poor. They were rich. They were good stewards of their meager resources. They produced abundance at a time of deprivation and poverty.

It is my greatest hope that you will tread gently on this earth and tend your garden well. I pray your frugality will not become a romance with money for that is a pitiful, cold existence. Money is a frigid lover. When King Midas' touch turned his daughter into a statue of solid gold, she was no comfort in his old age. Do you doubt the truth of the scripture, "The root of all evil is the love of money"?

THE COMPLETION OF A FRUGAL PHILOSOPHY IS EMBRACING THE JOY OF GIVING! This joy is found in experiencing the paradox of receiving through giving. It's mysterious and ultimately illogical, unexplainable, but profoundly true. That may be why so many extremely wealthy people seek philanthropy (giving money away) as an occupation with more satisfaction than actually earning money.

That is why the only place in Bible where God tells us to test him in His promise to us is when He tells us to "tithe" or give back to Him the first 10% of our income. He says in Malachi, 3:10 "Bring all the tithes into the storehouse.... If you do," says the Lord Almighty, "I will open the windows of heaven for you. I will pour out a blessing so great you won't have enough room to take it in! Try it! Let me prove it to you!" NLT

In closing this book, I want you to ponder what I believe to be the main reason to be frugal in your spending. It is so that out of the surplus of your frugality, you can be frivolous in your giving. Don't die with any money in your pockets, because it won't be worth anything where you're going! Don't try to figure it out, just count it all joy to be blessed by giving.

BONUS REFERENCE GUIDE

IMPORTANT BOOKS (must read books are in **BOLD**)

SHOP, SAVE AND SHARE
by Ellie Kay
Bethany House, 1998
(Best book for coupon super shopping and giving to others)

Debt-Free Living: How to get out of Debt (and Stay Out)
by Larry Burkett
Moody Press, 2000 (revised)
(America's best budgeting authority)

Die Broke
by Stephen M. Pollan and Mark Levine
Harper Business
(A radical new look at retirement income and giving; don't miss it!)

The Only Investment Guide You'll Ever Need
by Andrew Tobias
Harcourt Brace & Company 1998 (revised)

Master Your Money: A Step by Step for Financial Freedom
by Ron Blue
Thomas Nelson Publishers, 1997 (revised)

The Tightwad Gazette, I II & III
by Amy Dacyczyn
Random House

Debt Proof Living
by Mary Hunt
Broadman and Holman, 2000

How to Save Money Everyday
by Ellie Kay
Bethany House 2001

The Late Start Investor
by John F. Wasik
Henry Holt & Co. 1998

Living Cheaply with Style
by Ernest Callenbach
Ronin Publisher, Inc.

1000 Ways to Cut Your Expenses
by Jonathon D. Pond

The Complete – How to Figure It – Book
by Darrell Huff
W.W. Norton & Co.

Practical Problem Solver
the Reader's Digest Association

The Consumers Bible
by Mark Green
Workman Publishing, New York

Second Hand Super Shopper
by Ellen Weiss
M. Evans & Co., Inc.

The Ultimate Householders Book
by Editor's of Consumer's Guide
A & W Publishing

Seven Keys for Doubling Your Standard of Living
by Noah Fuhrman
Collier Books, New York

Cheap Eating
by Pat Edwards
Upper Access, Inc.

FRUGAL WEBSITES

www.elliekay.com

www.thefrugalshopper.com

www.frugalmoms.com

www.frugalgazette.com

www.frugalliving.about.com

www.frugalfamilynetwork.com

www.frugalfun.com

www.thefrugallife.com

www.frugalhomemaker.com

COUPON WEBSITES

www.valpak.com

www.hotcoupons.com

www.(put any brand here).com

www.cents-off.com

www.elliekay.com

CREDIT CARDS THAT PAY YOU

Discover 800-347-2683

American Airlines 800-FLY-444

United Airlines 800-537-7783

American Express Miles Program 800-THE-CARD

Diners Club miles on all airlines 800-234-6377

5% for new cars:

General Motors 800-947-1000

Ford 800-285-3000

LOW COST AIRLINE TICKETS

www.Hotwire.com

www.Orbitz.com

www.Priceline.com or 800-PRICELINE

www.bestfares.com

www.Expedia.com

www.Travelocity.com

www.Travelweb.com

www.Cheaptickets.com

www.Smartliving.com

www.Southwest.com

RECREATIONAL VEHICHLE (RV) LIFESTYLE INFORMATION

Escapees RV Club
100 Rainbow Drive
Livingston, TX 77351
888-757-2582

www.escapees.com

Good Sam RV Owners Club
www.Goodsamclub.com

800-293-5177

Camping World – Presidents Club
P.O. Box 90017
Bowling Green, KY 42102-9017
800-626-5944
www.campingworld.com

CAR BUYING HELP

www.auto-by-tel.com

www.carclub.com 800-CAR-CLUB

Car Bargains 800-475-7283 (checkbook.org)

www.Cars.com

www.Edmunds.com

LIFE INSURANCE QUOTES

Wholesale Insurance Network (WIN) 800-808-5810

Insurance Quote Service 800-972-1104

WHOLE LIFE POLICY EVALUATION

Contact: James Hunt-Consumer Federation of America
                  Insurance Group
                  8 Tahanto St.
                  Concord, NH 03301

GENERAL INSURANCE QUOTES

Select Quote 800-350-0100

www.insureme.com

www.quotesmith.com

www.insure.com

www.quicken.com

HOME AND AUTO LOANS

www.hsh.com

www.bankrate.com

www.banx.com

www.homeshark.com - refinancing options

LEGAL CONSULTING

www.nolo.com

www.legaldocs.com

TELEPHONE SERVICE SHOPPING

www.Teleworth.com

HELP WITH COLLEGE TUITION

Federal Student Financial Aid Info Center 800-433-3243

HOTEL BARGAINS

www.Hotwire.com

www.Travelweb.com

www.Priceline.com

Hotel Reservations Network 800-643-6835

RESTAURANT DISCOUNT CARDS

Trans Media Card   (20% at selected restaurants)
www.transmediacard.com   800-422-5090

IGT (In Good Taste) 25 %
www.igtcard.com 800-444-8872

SELECTED DISCOUNT BROKERS

Ameritrade	800-669-3900
Charles Schwab & Co.	800-435-4000
E*Trade	800-786-2575
Fidelity Brokerage	800-544-8666
Kennedy Cabot	800-252-0090
Jack White	800-233-3411
Muriel Siebert	800-872-0444
National Discount Brokers	800-417-7423
Quick & Reilly	800-221-5220
Vanguard Discount Brokerage	800-992-8327
Waterhouse Securities	800-934-4410

STOP TELEPHONE SOLICITATION

Send name, address and phone # to:

Telephone Preference Service
Direct Marketing Association
P.O. Box 9014
Farmingdale, NY 11735

STOP JUNK MAIL

Send all variations of your name & address to:

Mail Preference Service
Direct Marketing Association
P.O. Box 9008
Farmingdale, NY 11735

STOP UNSOLICITED CREDIT CARD APPLICATIONS

Call 1-800-353-0809 Automated system, may take up to 3 months for results

GARDENING SEEDS

Fedco Seeds
P.O. Box 250-A
Waterville, ME 04903
www.Fedcoseeds.com

FREE GOVERNMENT CONSUMER PUBLICATIONS

For catalog write to:

Consumer Information Center –2D
P.O. box 100
Pueblo, CO 81002

FREE BUSINESS ADVICE

Call SCORE 800-634-0245

TOLL FREE NUMBER DIRECTORY ASSISTANCE

800-555-1212

RESTAURANT COUPONS

www.valpak.com

www.citysearch.com

www.(restaurant's name).com

FREE MAPS ON THE INTERNET

www.mapquest.com

www.mapblast.com

www.mapsonus.comw

ww.interstate4U.com

STATE TOURISM OFFICES

Go to Travel Industry Association @ www.tia.org

WEATHER INFORMATION

www.weather.com

www.accuweather.com

www.worldclimate.com

INTERNET AUCTIONS FOR TRAVEL

www.ebay.com

www.boxlott.com

www.skyauction.com

www.bidtripper.com

DAY TRIP DESTINATIONS

www.bestsmalltowns.com

CHECK YOUR CREDIT REPORT

Equifax 800-685-1111

Experian 888-297-3741

Trans Union 800-888-4213 (Costs Approx. $8.00)

CREDIT HELP/FINANCIAL COUNSELING

Crown Financial Ministries
P.O. Box 100
Gainesville, GA 30503-0100
www.crown.org (best site for budget info)

Trinity Credit Counselors
800-758-3844

www.trinitycredit.org

National Foundation for Consumer Credit
800-388-2277

www.nfcc.org

Debt Counselors of America
800-680-3328
www.dca.org

Debt Relief Clearinghouse
800-433-2843

www.debtreliefonline.com

PREPAID COLLEGE TUITION PLANS BY STATE

877-277-6496 or collegesavings.org

COLLEGE SCHOLARSHIPS RESEARCH

National Scholarship Research Service
5577 Skylande Blvd. Suite 6A
Santa Rosa, CA 95403
707-546-6777
www.800headstart.com

CHRISTIAN MEDICAL INSURANCE ALTERNATIVES

Christian Care Medi-Share
800-374-2562
www.med-share.org

Samaritan Ministries
877-764-2436
www.samaritanministries.org

Christian Brotherhood Newsletter
800-791-6225
www.cbnews.org

MEDICAL BILL REDUCTION NEGOTIATORS

The Karis Group
Medical Bill Help
866-245-5435
www.thekarisgroup.com

MONTHLY SAVINGS PAYMENET NECESSARY TO ACHIEVE $1 MILLION VALUE AT VARIOUS INTEREST RATES AND TIME-PERIODS, COMPOUNDED MONTHLY.

TIME	Interest Rate 4%	Interest Rate 5%	Interest Rate 6%	Interest Rate 7%	Interest Rate 8%	Interest Rate 9%	Interest Rate 10%	Interest Rate 11%	Interest Rate 12%	Interest Rate 13%	Interest Rate 14%	Interest Rate 15%
10 yrs	$6,791.18	$6,439.88	$6,102.05	$5,777.51	$5,466.09	$5,167.58	$4,881.74	$4,608.33	$4,347.09	$4,097.74	$3,859.98	$3,633.50
15 yrs	$4,063.55	$3,741.27	$3,438.57	$3,154.95	$2,889.85	$2,642.67	$2,412.72	$2,199.30	$2,011.68	$1,819.09	$1,650.75	$1,495.87
20 yrs	$2,726.47	$2,432.89	$2,164.31	$1,919.66	$1,697.73	$1,497.26	$1,316.88	$1,155.22	$1,010.86	$882.42	$768.54	$667.90
25 yrs	$1,945.04	$1,6679.23	$1,443.01	$1,234.46	$1,051.50	$891.96	$753.67	$634.46	$532.24	$445.02	$370.95	$308.31
30 yrs	$1,440.82	$1,201.54	$995.51	$819.69	$670.98	$546.00	$442.38	$356.56.	$285.13	$228.66	$182.05	$144.44
35 yrs	$1,094.41	$880.21	$701.89	$555.23	$435.94	$339.92	$263.39	$202.91	$155.50	$118.60	$90.07	$68.13
40 yrs	$846.05	$655.30	$502.14	$380.98	$286.45	$213.61	$158.13	$116.27	$84.99	$61.80	$44.73	$32.24
45 yrs	$662.48	$493.48	$362.85	$263.67	$189.59	$135.05	$95.39	$66.89	$46.61	$32.29	$22.26	$15.28
50 yrs	$523.74	$374.72	$264.05	$183.55	$126.08	$85.70	$57.72	$38.57	$25.60	$16.89	$11.09	$7.25

* To achieve $500,000 value, divide payment by 2.

TOTAL VALUE ACHIEVED WHEN SAVING $250 PER MONTH ($3,000 PER YEAR) CALUCULATED AT VARIOUS INTEREST RATES AND TIME PERIODS, COMPOUNDED DAILY

TIME PERIOD	Interest Rate 4%	Interest Rate 5%	Interest Rate 6%	Interest Rate 7%	Interest Rate 8%	Interest Rate 9%	Interest Rate 10%	Interest Rate 11%	Interest Rate 12%	Interest Rate 13%	Interest Rate 14%	Interest Rate 15%
5 yrs	$16,577	$17,055	$17,449	$17,907	$18,381	$18,872	$19,379	$19,905	$20,449	$21,012	$21,595	$22,198
10 yrs	$36,824	$38,841	$41,002	$43,318	$45,802	$48,468	$51,329	$54,403	$57,706	$61,257	$65,076	$69,186
15 yrs	$61,555	$66,878	$72,794	$79,376	$86,707	$94,771	$104,002	$114,192	$125,587	$138,340	$152,626	$168,643
20 yrs	$91,760	$102,878	$115,708	$130,544	$147,728	$167,667	$190,839	$217,814	$249,261	$285,977	$328,905	$379,162
25 yrs	$128,638	$149,087	$173,606	$203,120	$238,727	$281,788	$334,000	$397,401	$474,588	$568,750	$683,840	$824,762
30 yrs	$173,712	$208,453	$251,827	$306,185	$374,550	$460,817	$570,015	$708,645	$885,121	$1,110,351	$1,398,495	$1,767,951
35 yrs	$228,747	$284,660	$357,372	$452,391	$577,120	$741,537	$959,112	$1,248,938	$1,633,086	$2,147,690	$2,837,441	$3,764,374
40 yrs	$295,267	$382,510	$499,839	$659,859	$879,306	$1,181,770	$1,600,580	$2,182,938	$2,995,833	$4,134,525	$5,734,733	$7,990,151
45 yrs	$378,068	$508,151	$692,145	$954,261	$1,330,095	$1,872,154	$2,658,110	$3,803,176	$5,478,674	$7,939,947	$11,568,381	$16,934,744
50 yrs	$478,346	$669,473	$951,724	$1,372,023	$2,002,564	$2,954,832	$4,401,563	$6,611,227	$10,002,261	$15,228,546	$23,314,322	$35,867,530

- When increasing your savings rate by $83/month ($1,000/year), multiply result by 1.333

MORTGAGE SAVINGS EXAMPLES WHEN APPLYING ONE EXTRA

PRINCIPLE & INTEREST PAYMENT MONTHLY OVER THE LIFE OF

THE LOAN

Total savings is the BOLD number in box
Extra monthly payment is second number in box

Mortgage
Principle   Interest Rate for a 30-year loan
amount

	6%	6.5%	7%	7.5%	8%
$100,000	**$39,270** $49.50	**$45,615** $52.67	**$49,937** $55.44	**$56,048** $58.27	**$62,692** $61.15
$150,000	**$58,906** $75.08	**$66,528** $79.01	**$74,906** $83.16	**$84,073** $87.40	**$93,489** $91.67
$200,000	**$78,541** $99.90	**$88,704** $104.35	**$99,874** $111.00	**$112,098** $116.54	**$126,207** $122.29

Mortgage
Principle   Interest Rate for a 15-year loan
amount

	6%	6.5%	7%	7.5%	8%
$100,000.	**$17,711** $70.25	**$19.170** $72.58	**$20,574** $74.90	**$21,979** $77.25	**$23,499** $79.64
$150,000.	**$26,910** $105.48	**$28,811** $108.89	**$30,820** $112.35	**$32,969** $115.88	**$35,249** $119.42
$200,000.	**$35,880** $140.64	**$38,415** $145.18	**$41,094** $149.81	**$43,958** $154.50	**$46,998** $159.28

EXAMPLES OF SAVINGS ON TOTAL PAYBACK ON 15-YEAR MORTGAGE VERSUS A 30-YEAR MORTGAGE

30-year payment is first number in box
15-year payment is underlined number in box
Savings is BOLD number in box

Mortgage Principle amount   **Interest Rate**

	6%	6.5%	7%	7.5%	8%
$100,000.	$599.55. $843.86 **$69,943.00**	$632.00 $871.11 **$70,720.00**	$665.30 $898.83 **$77,718.00**	$699.21 $927.01 **$84,853.00**	$733.73 $955.65 **$92,136.00**
$150,000.	$899.33 $1265.79 **$95,915.00**	$948.10 $1306.66 **$106,117.00**	$997.95 $1348.00 **$116.622.00**	$1,048.82 $1,390.52 **$127,281.00**	$11,100.65 $1,433.48 **$138,207.00**
$200,000.	$1,199.10 $1,687.71 **$127,888.00**	$1,264.14 $1,742.21 **$141,492.00**	$1,330.60 $1,797.66 **$155,437.00**	$1,398.60 $1,854.02 **$169,711.20**	$1,467.53 $1,911.30 **$184,276.00**